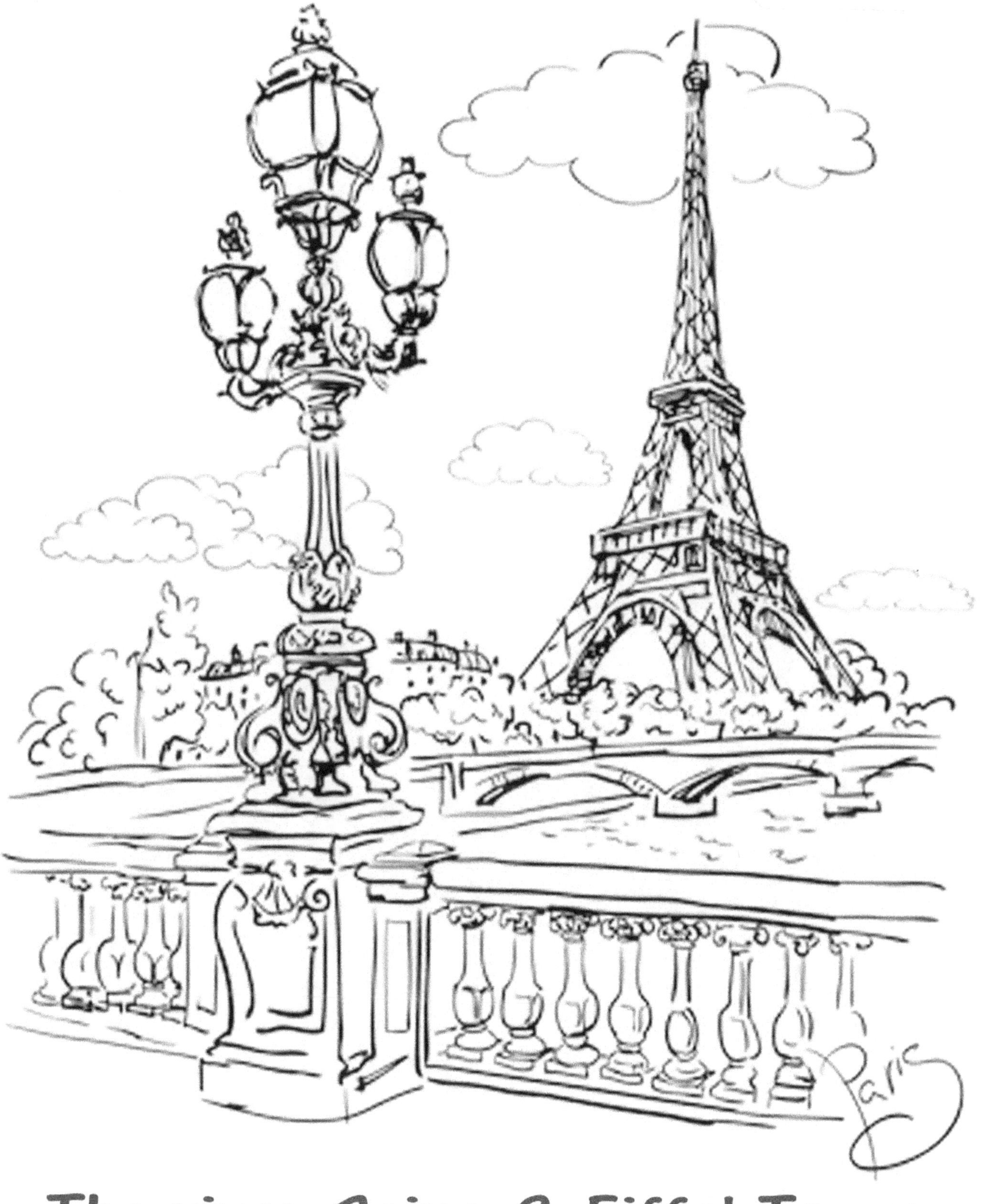

The river Seine & Eiffel Tower

Illustrated by:
Mandala & Caricature Illustration
Joshua Lazana Lagman and Jade Villaremo

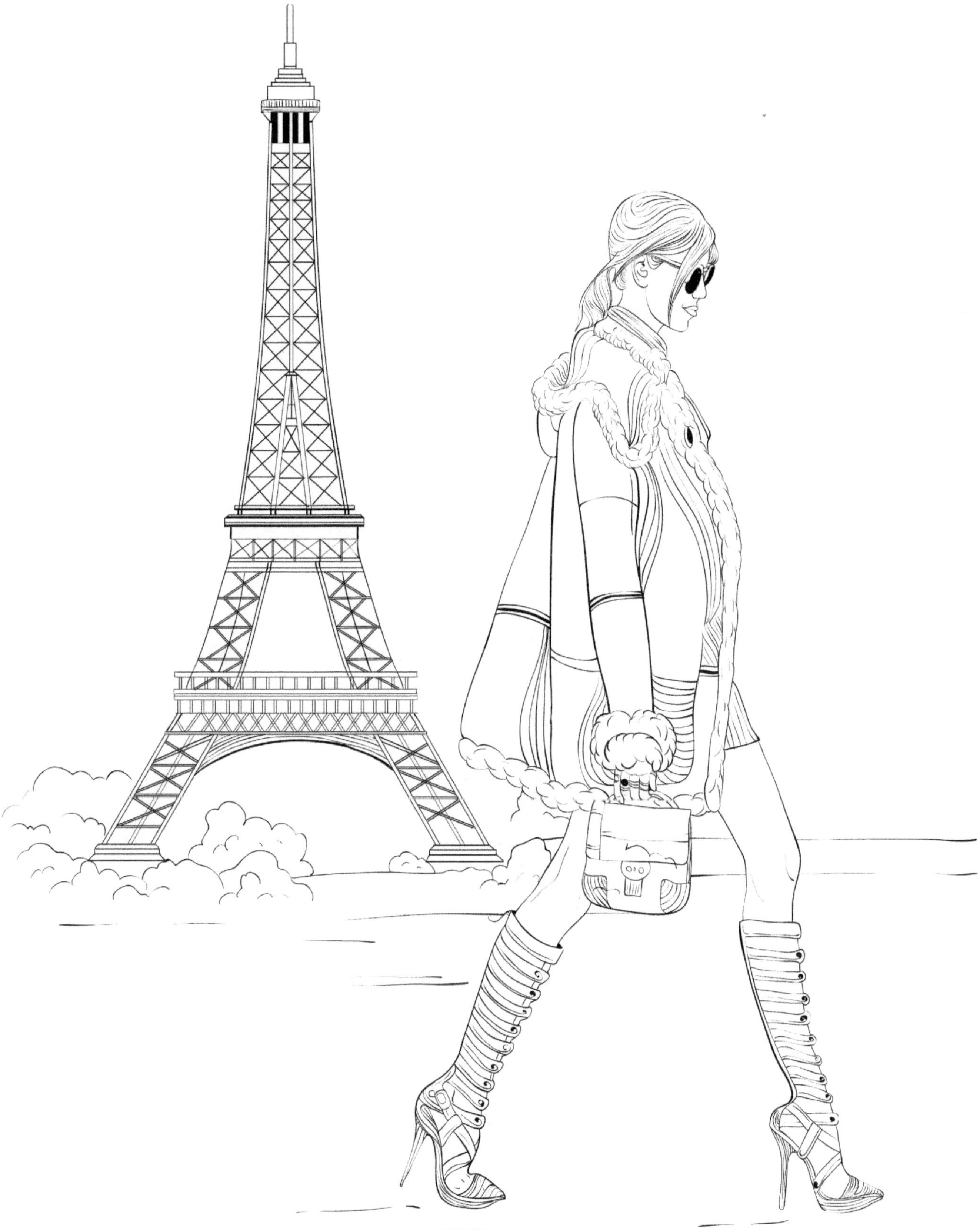

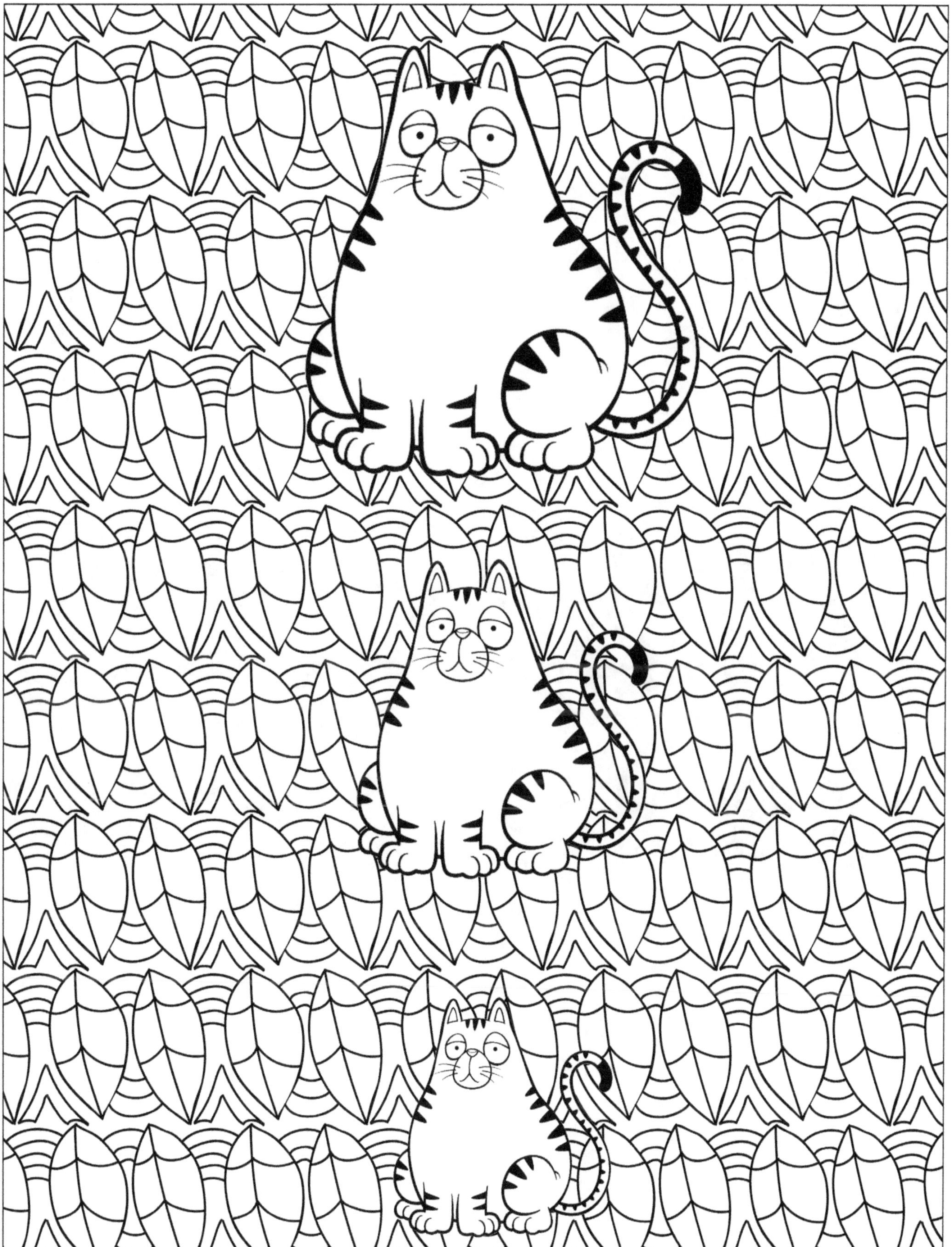

Montmartre

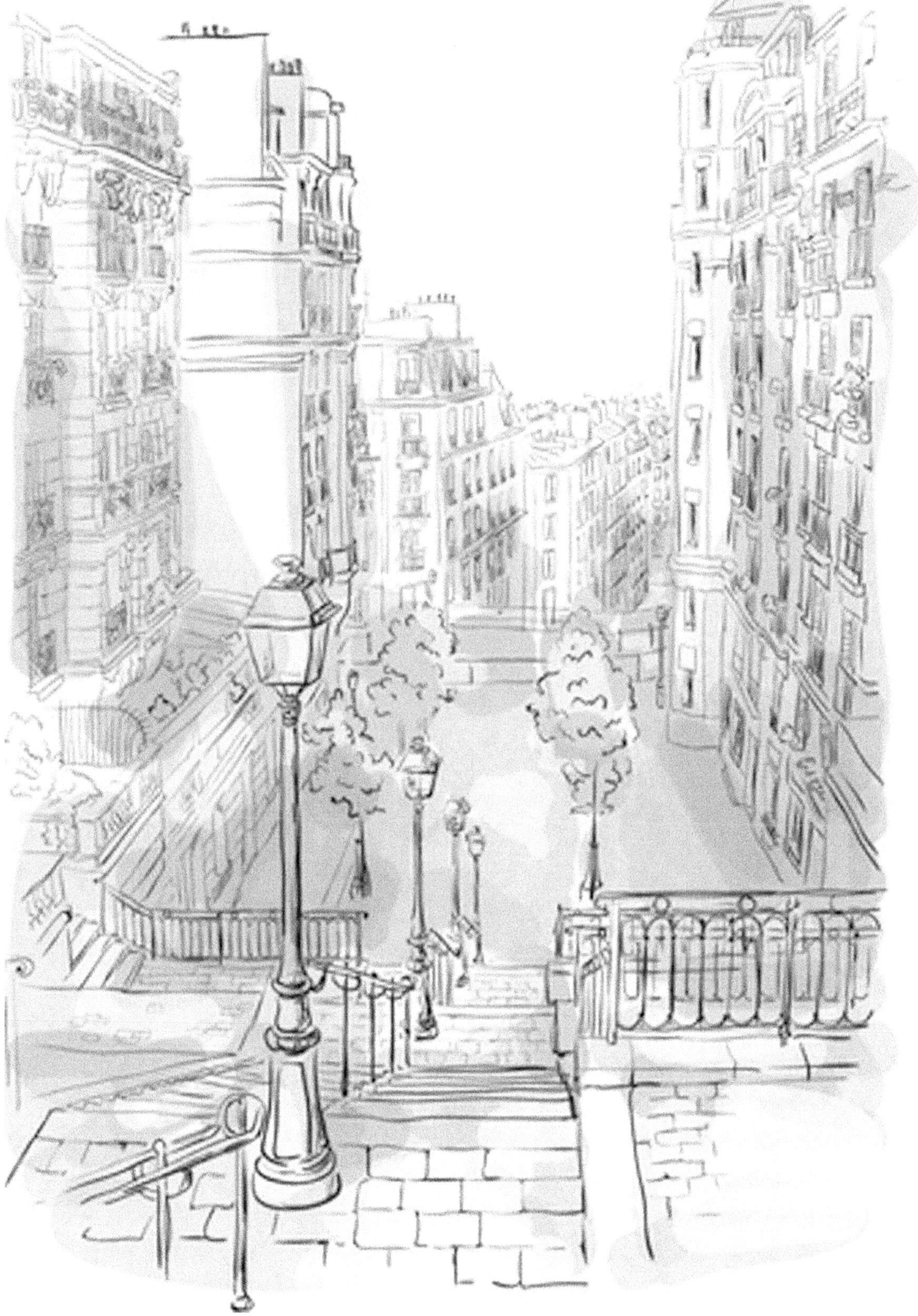

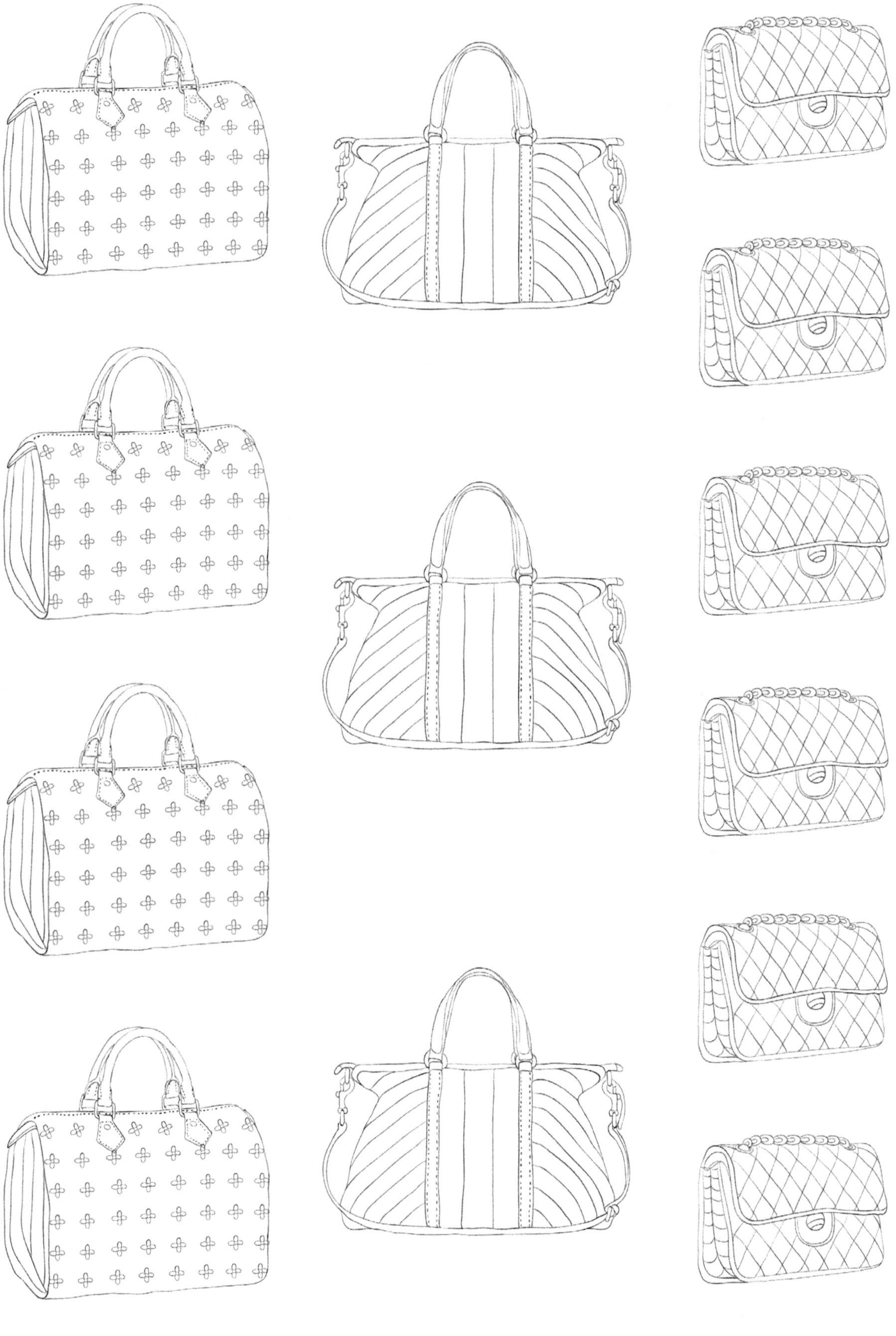

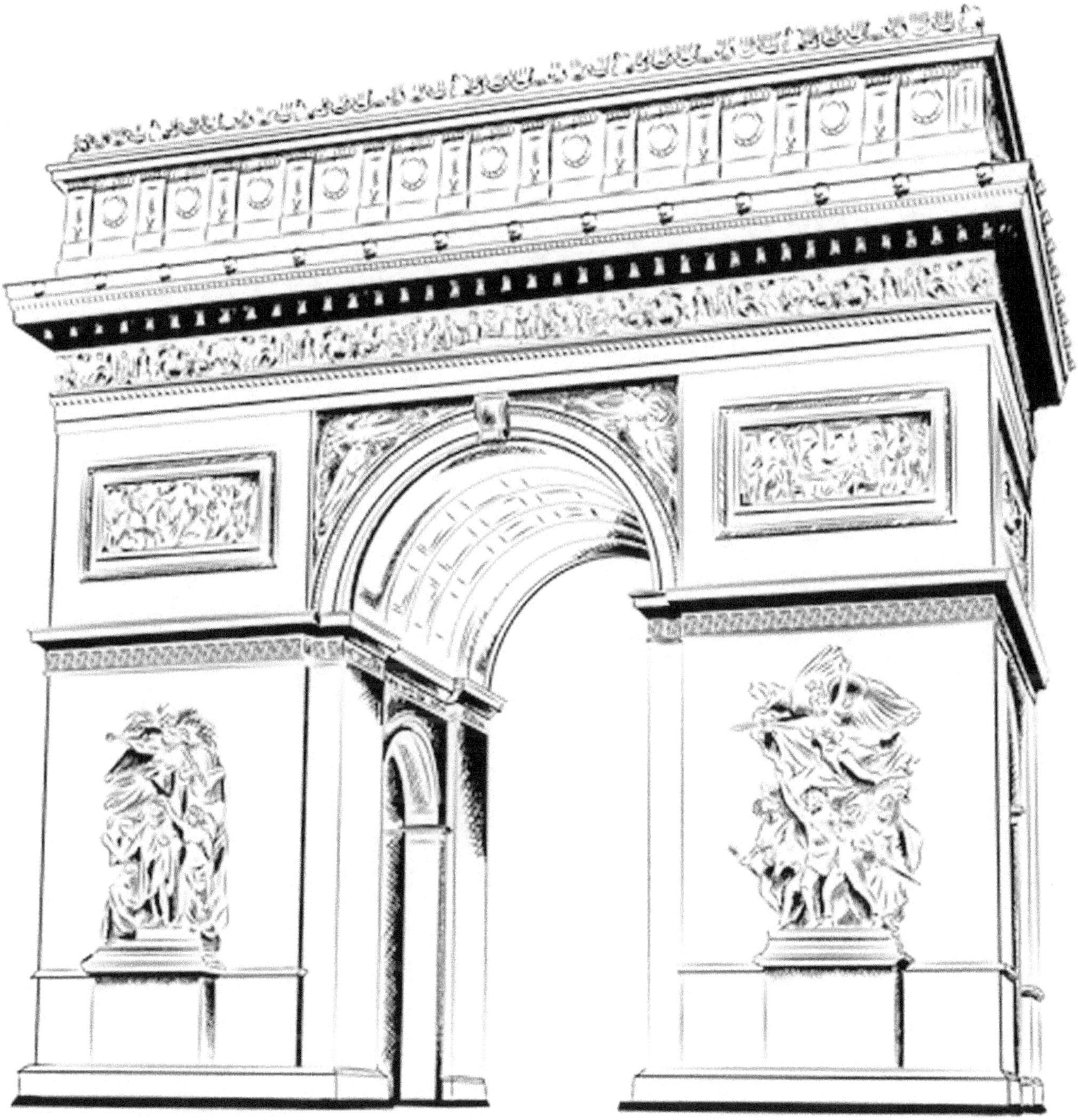

Triumph Arch

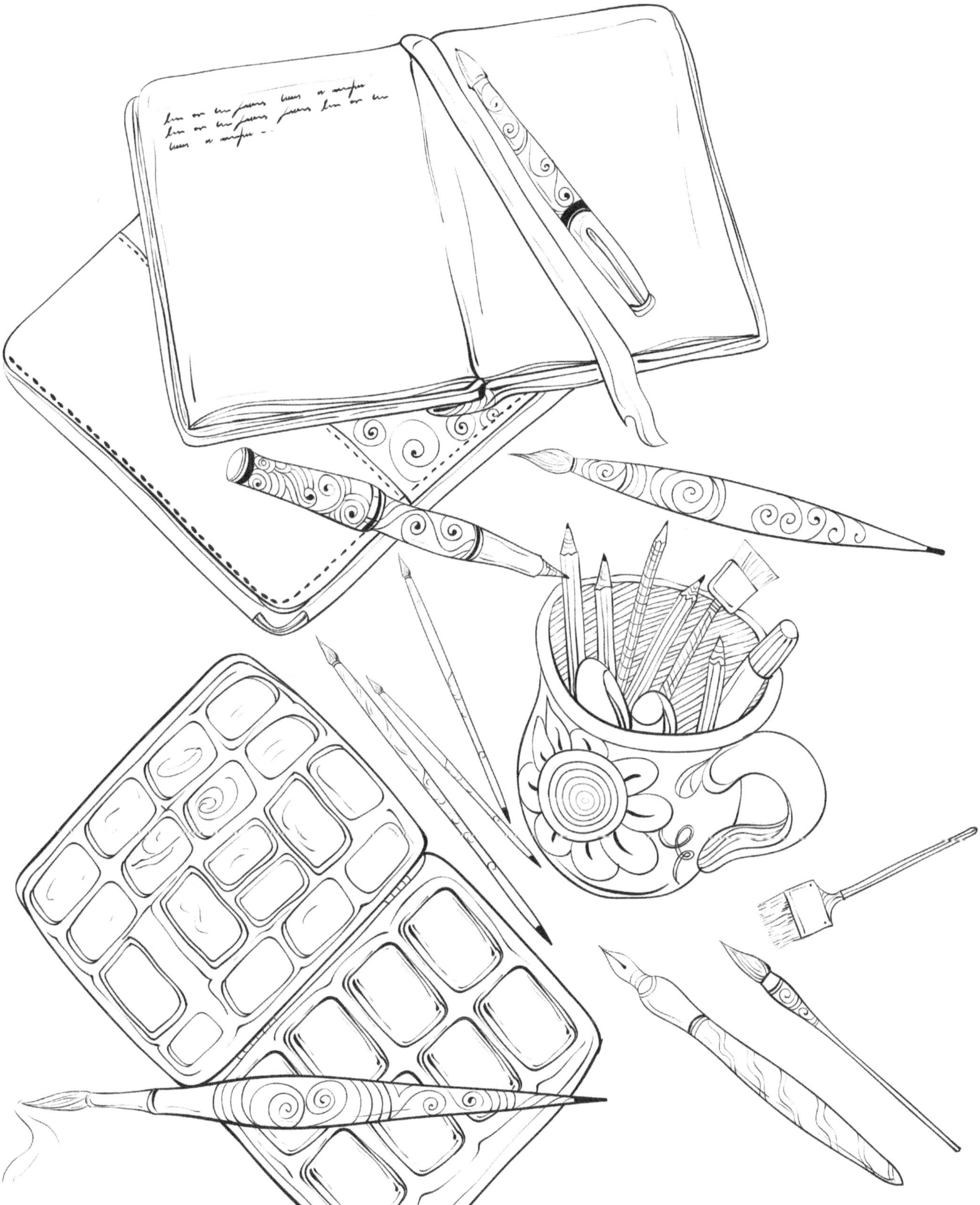

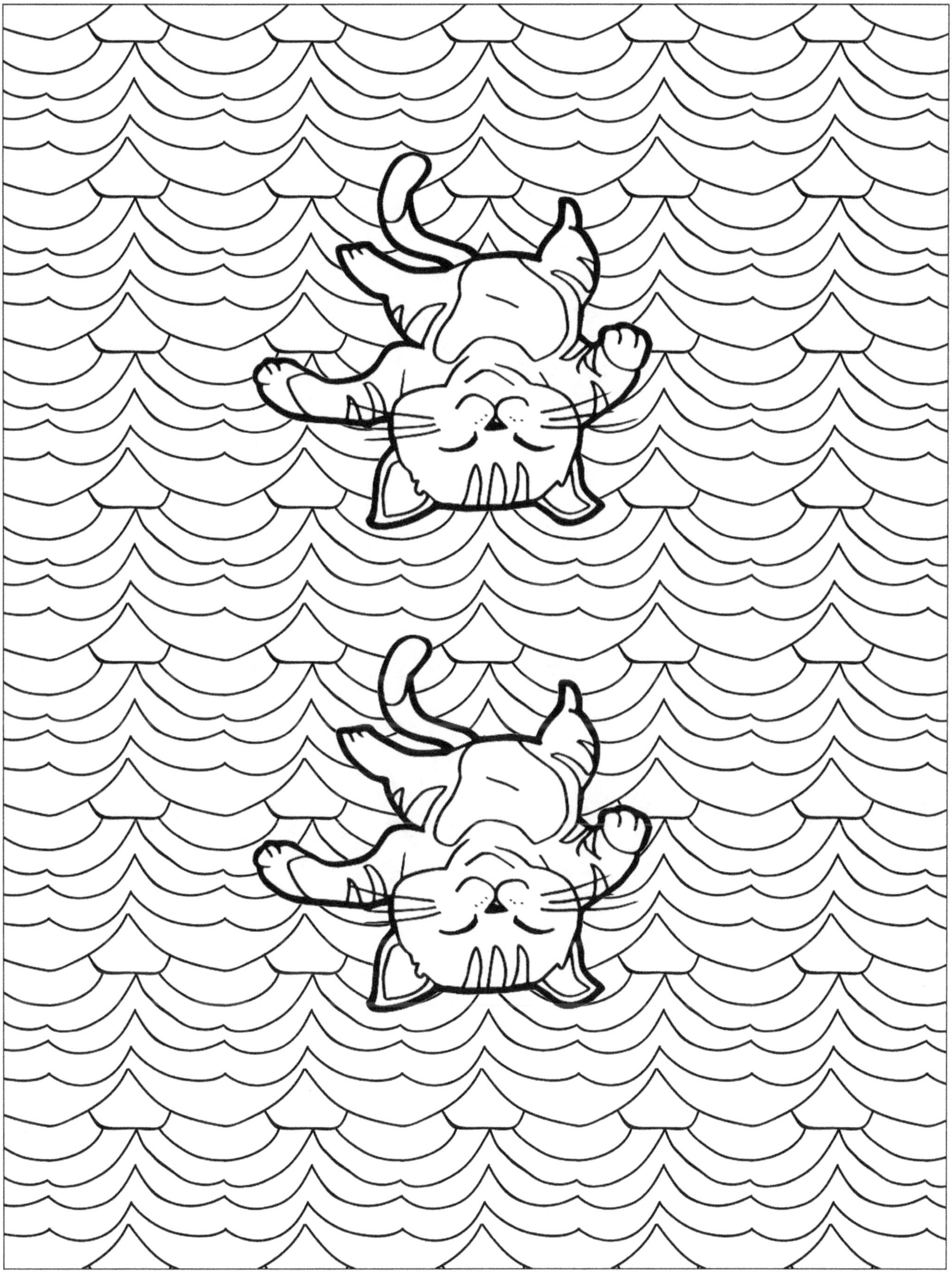

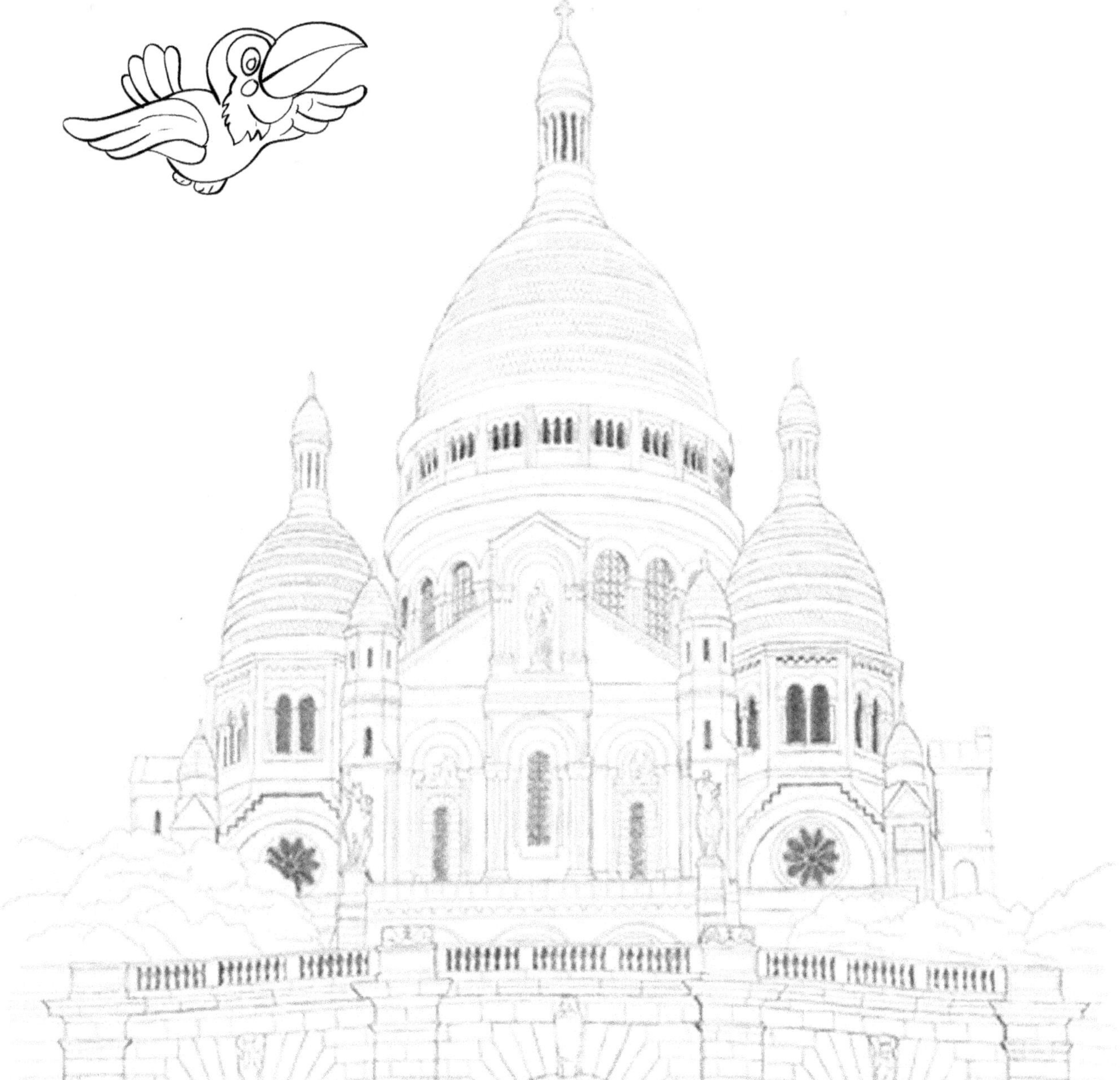

Sacre Coeur de Montmartre

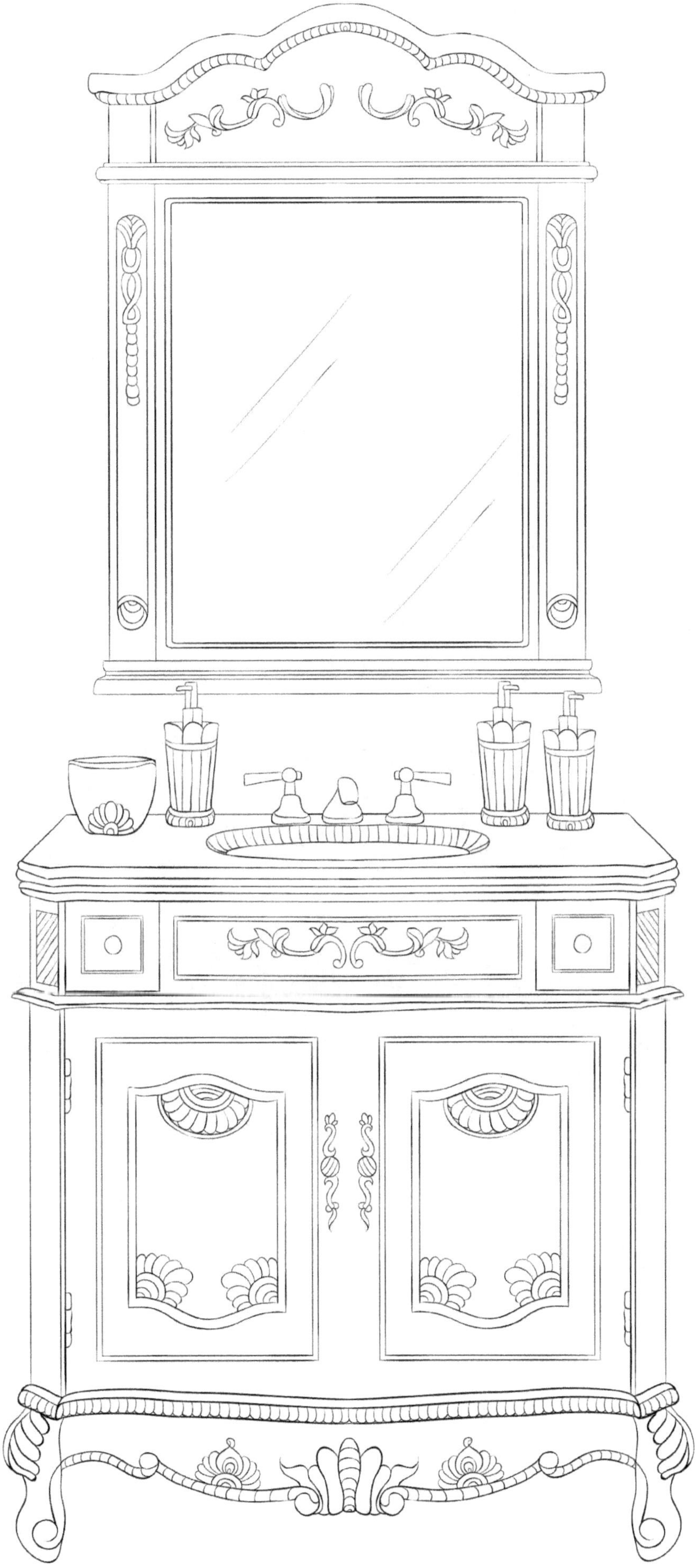

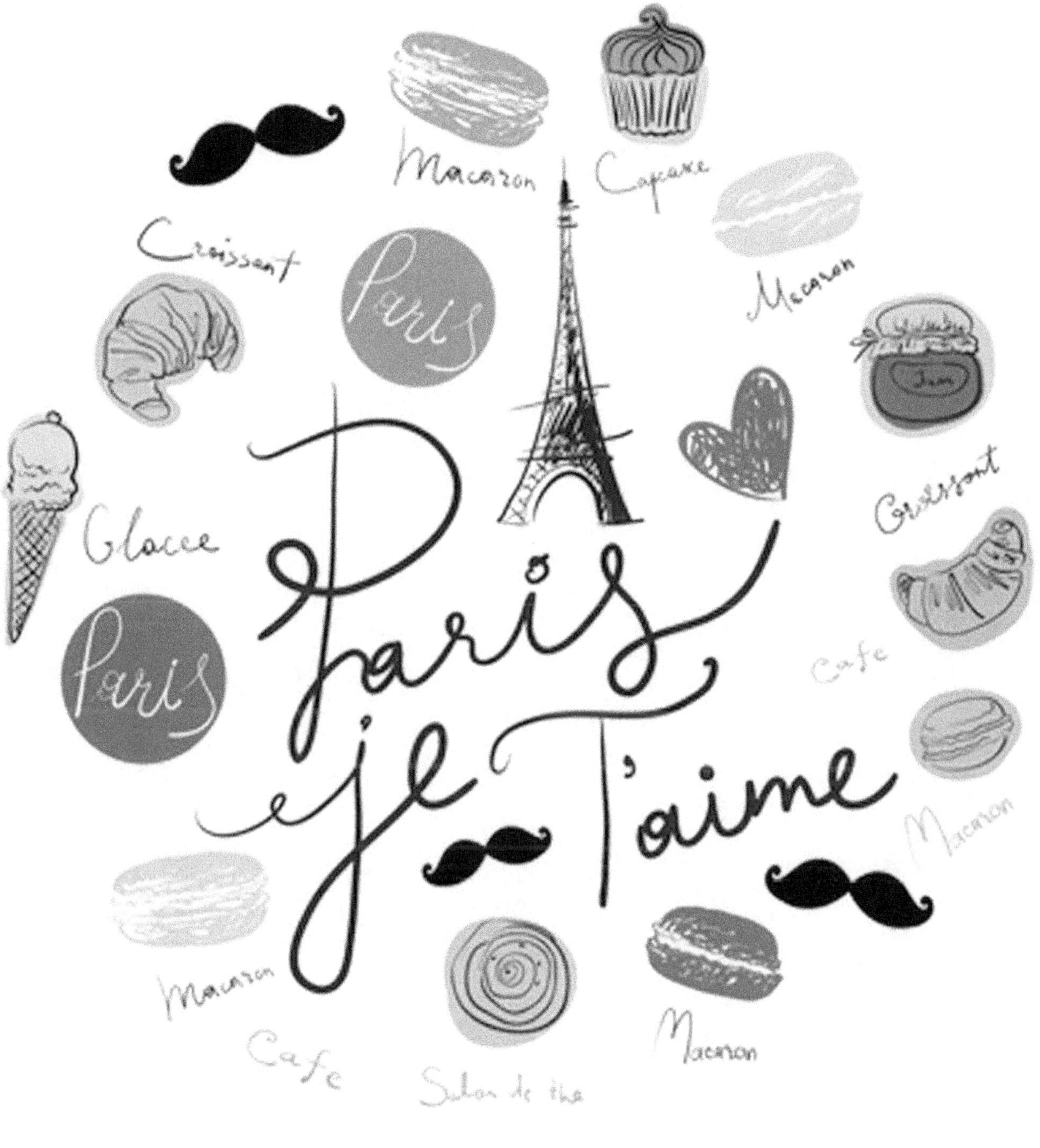
Macaron
Croissant
Paris
Macaron
Jam
Glacce
Paris
Paris je t'aime
Croissant
Cafe
Macaron
Macaron
Macaron
Cafe

BONJOUR

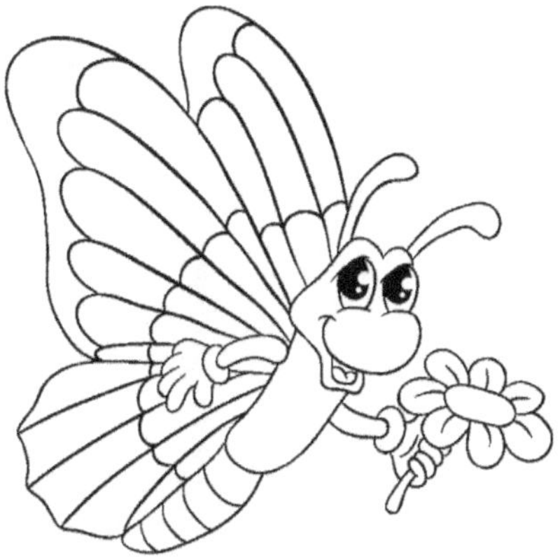
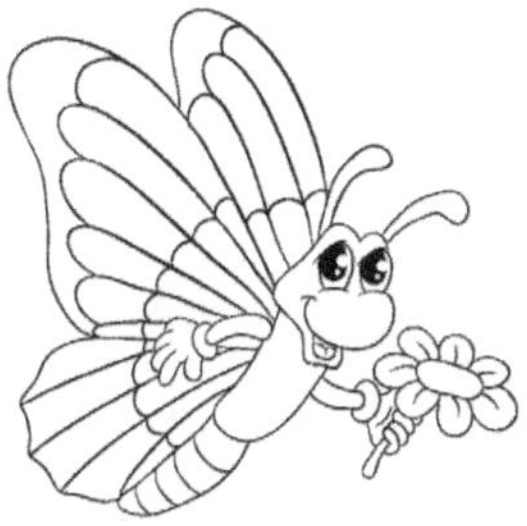
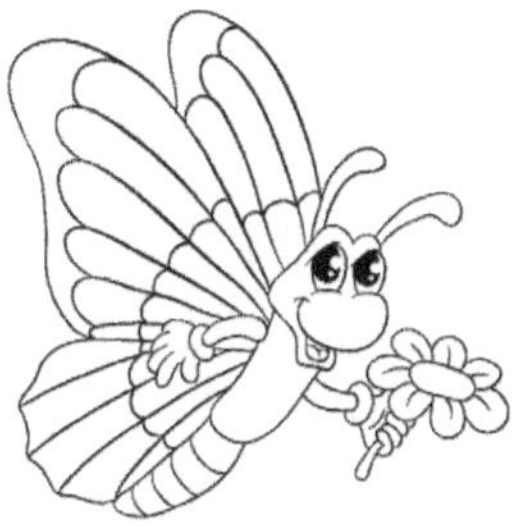
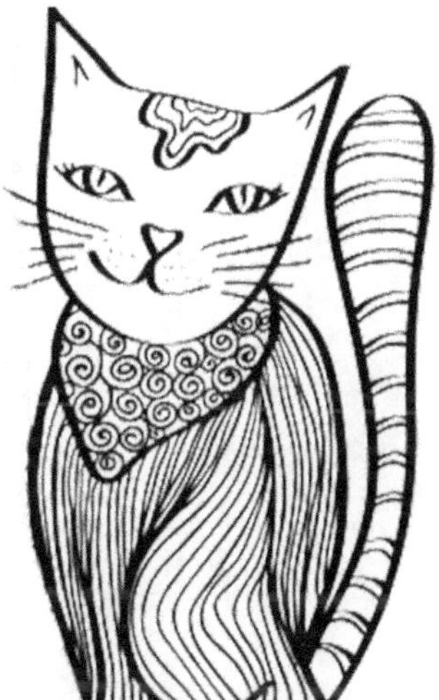
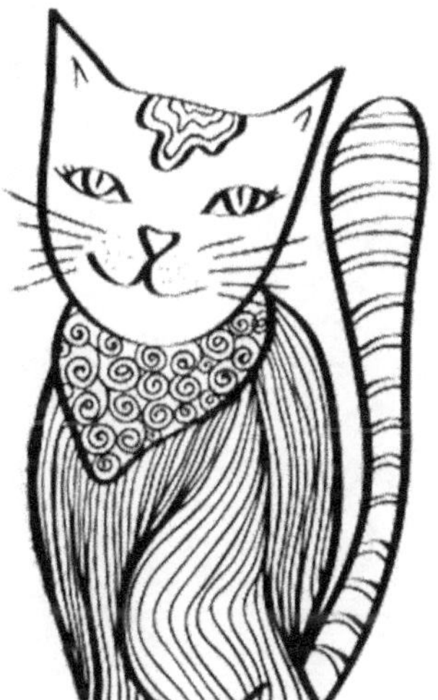
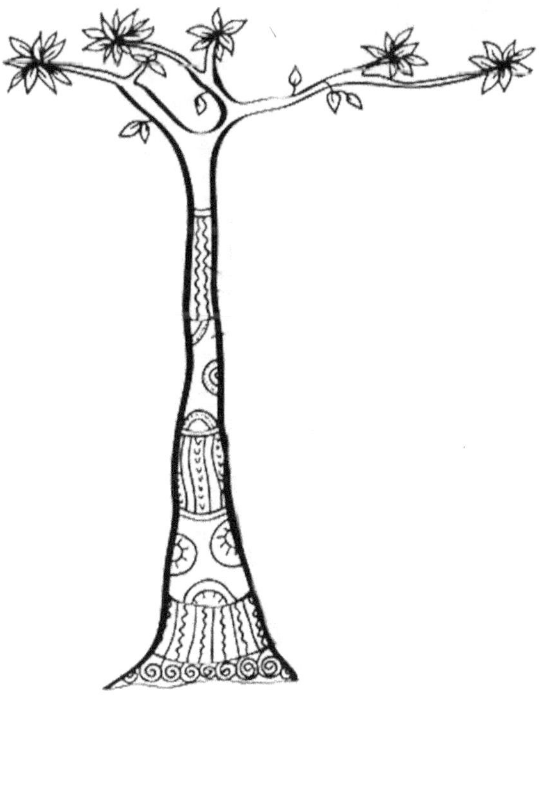
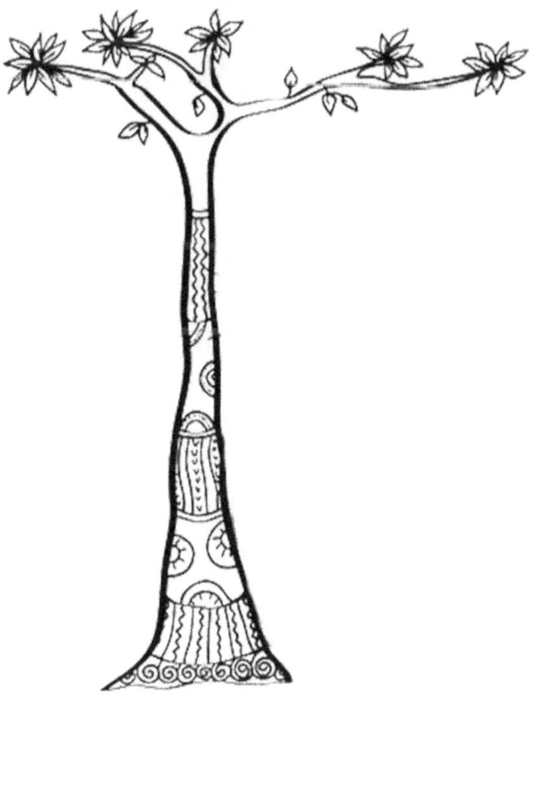

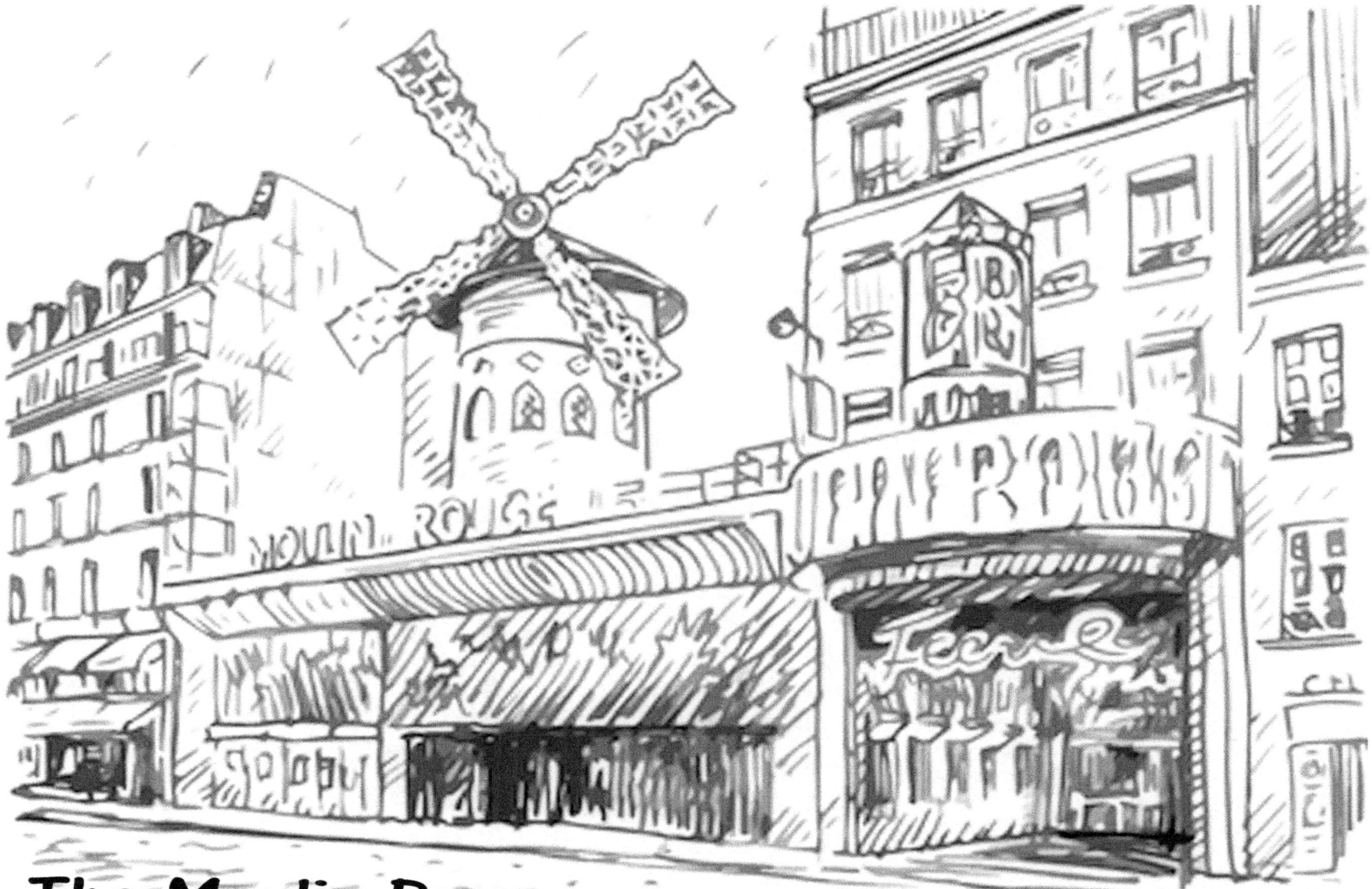

The Moulin Rouge

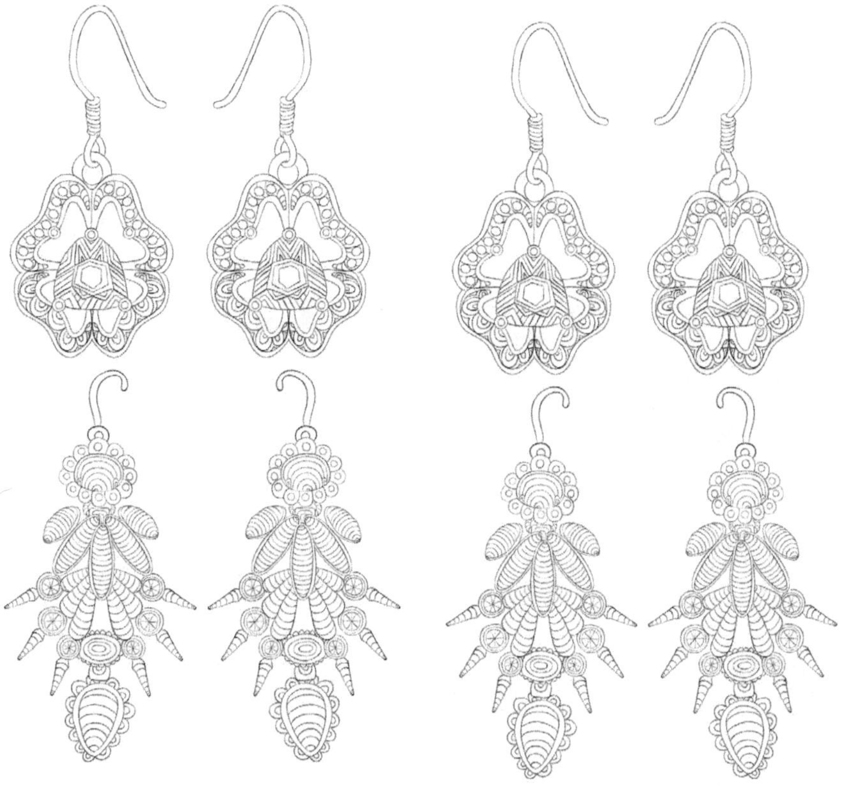

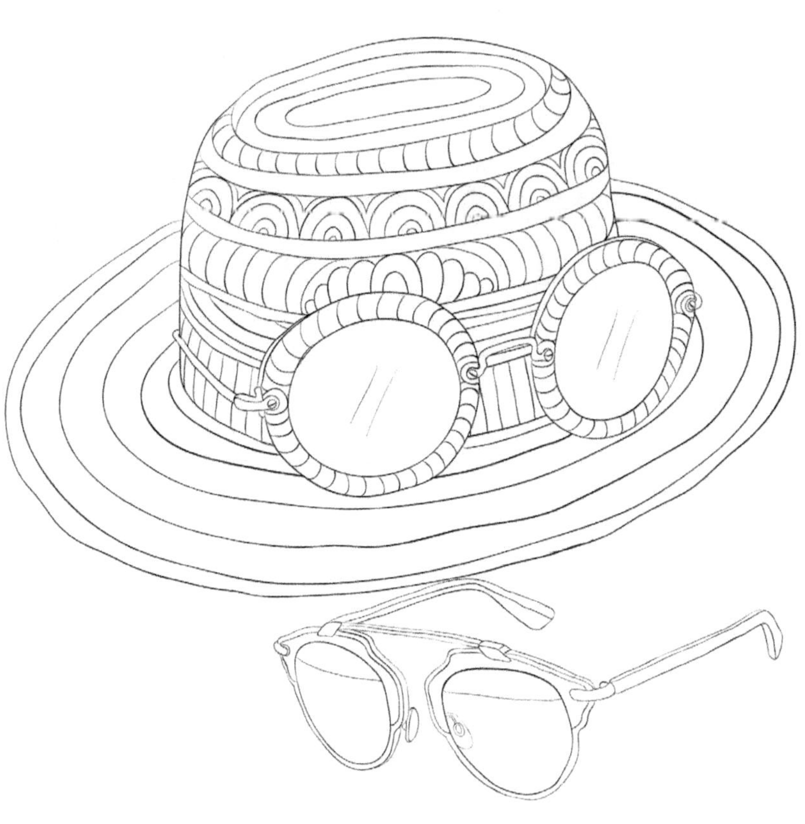

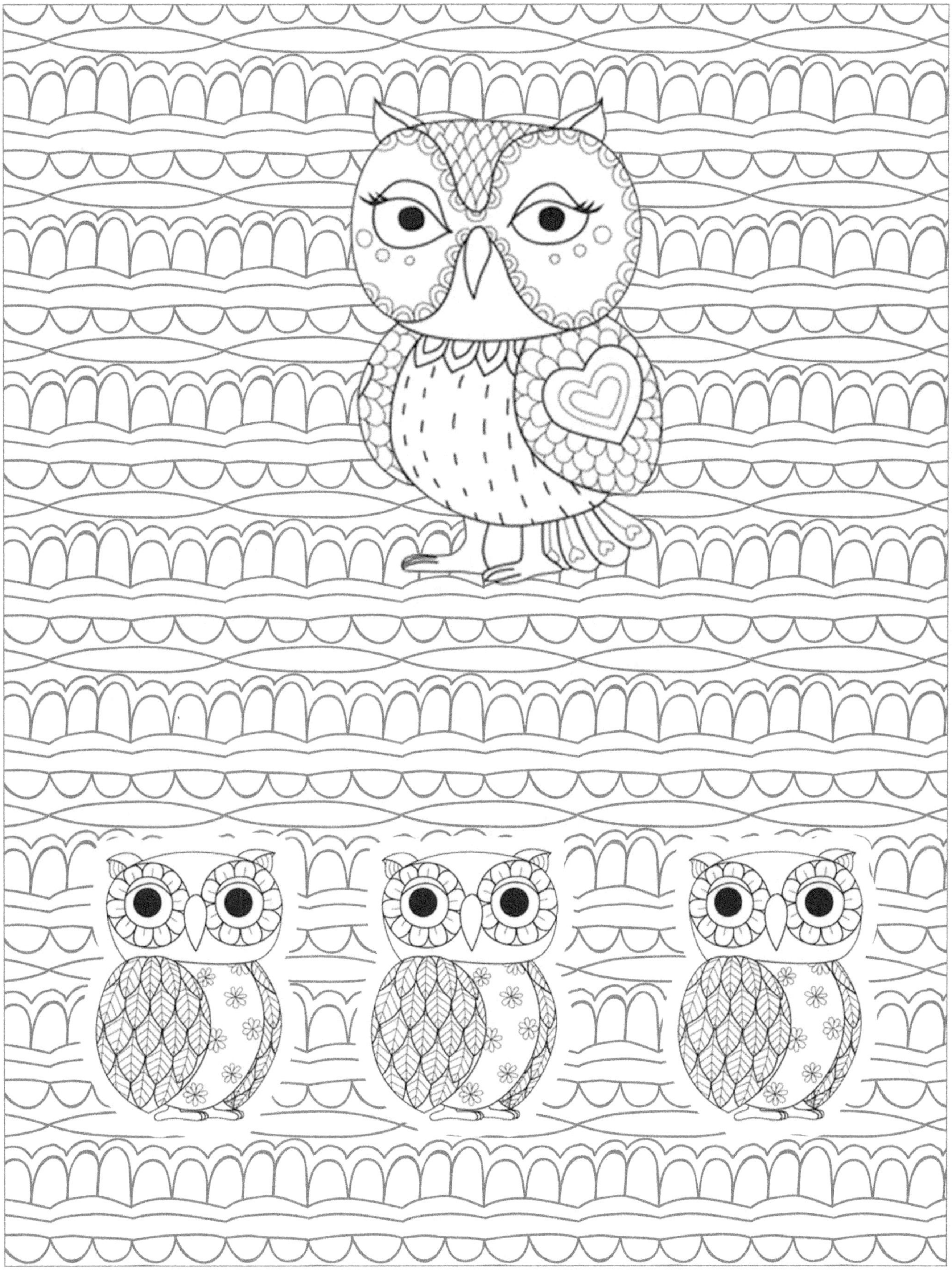

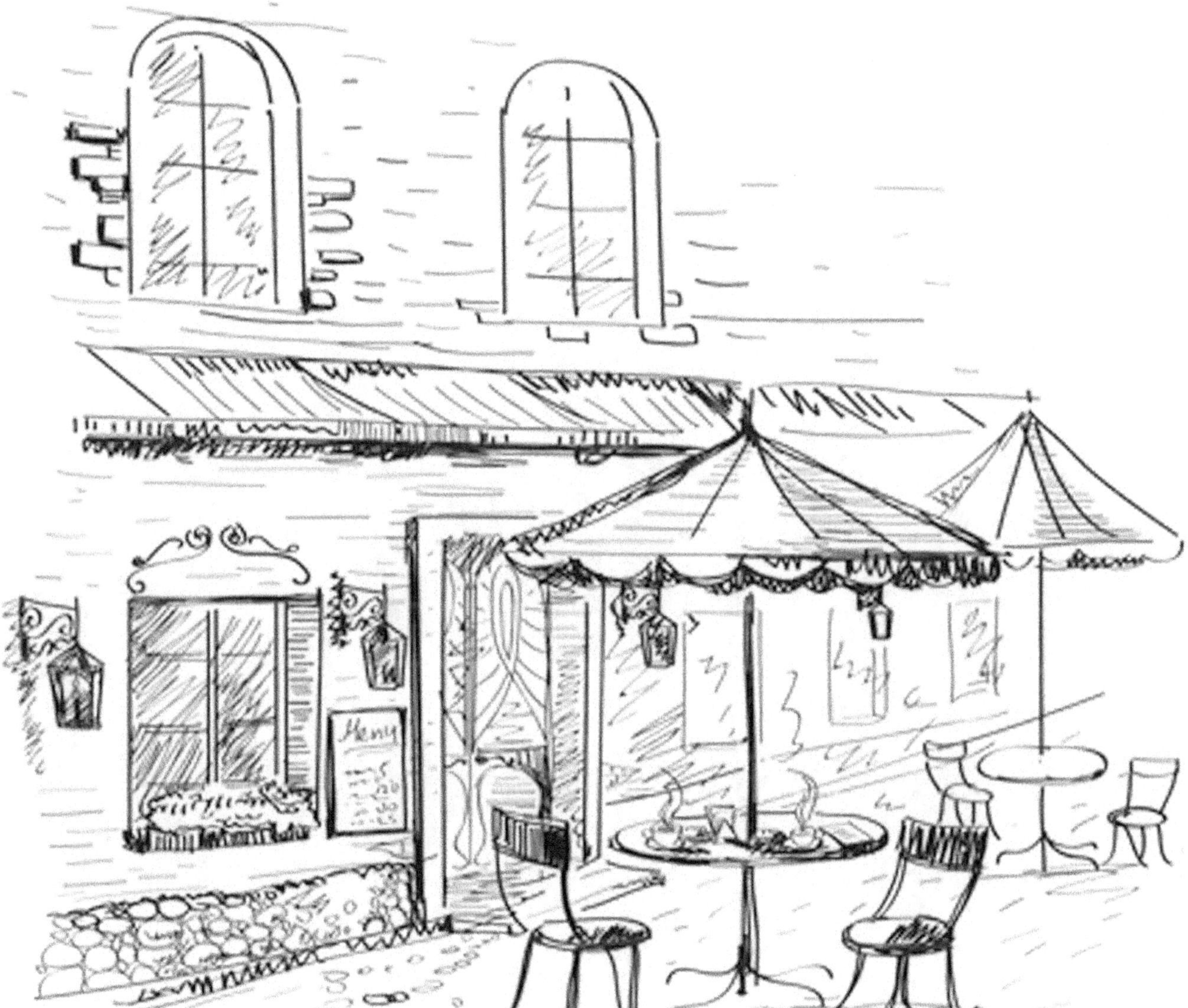
Menu

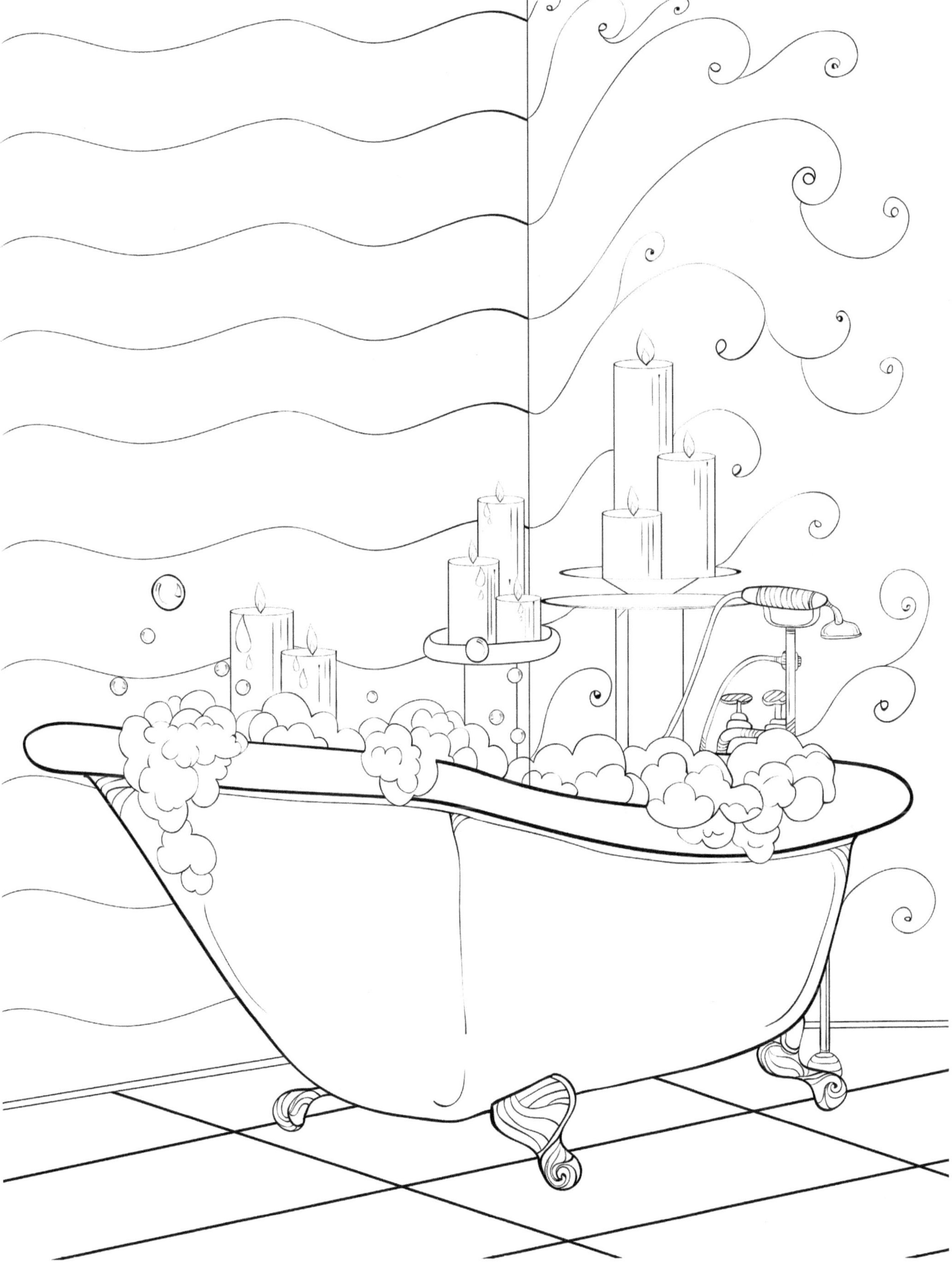

Bonjour
Fashion
Je t'aime
Paris

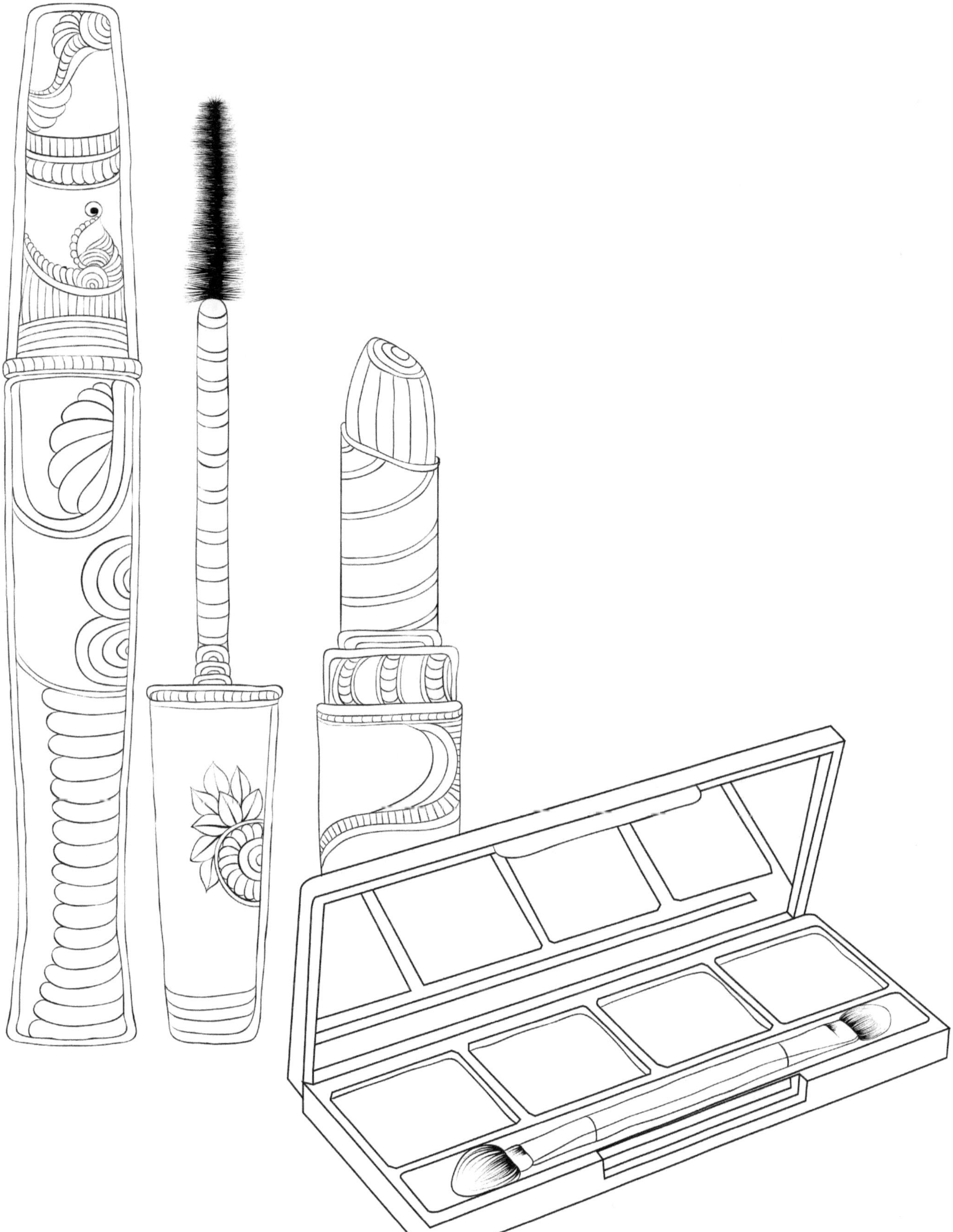

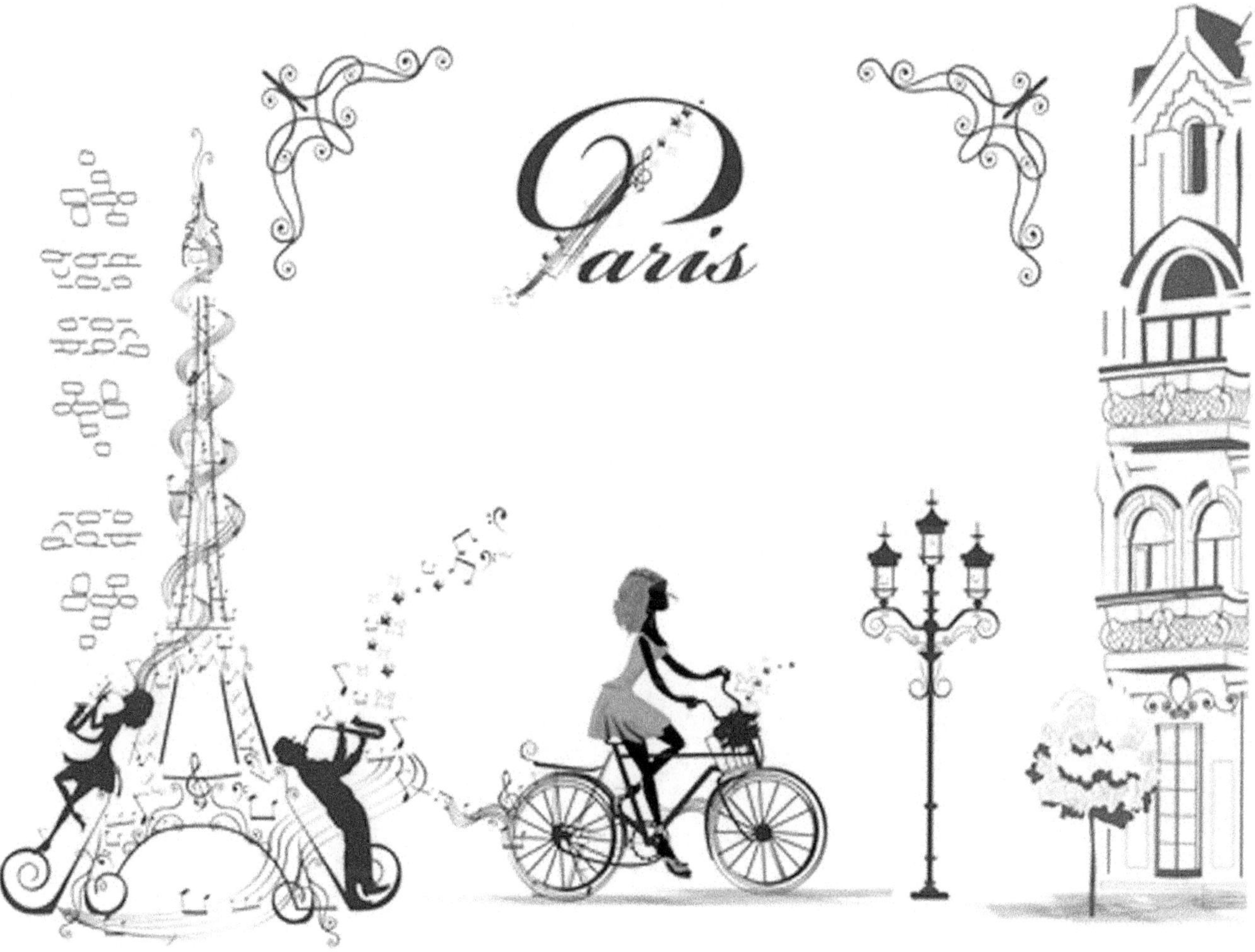
Paris

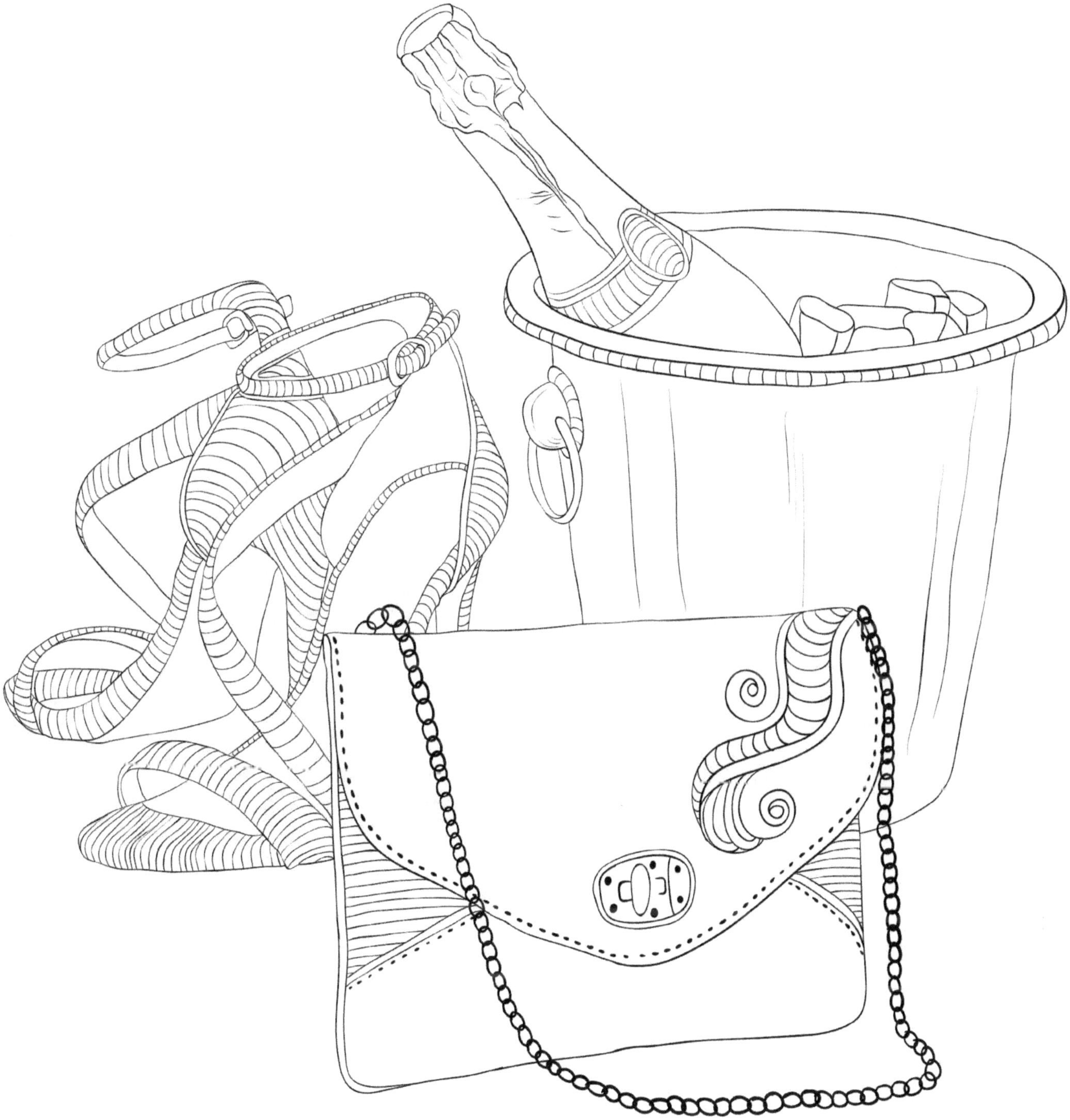

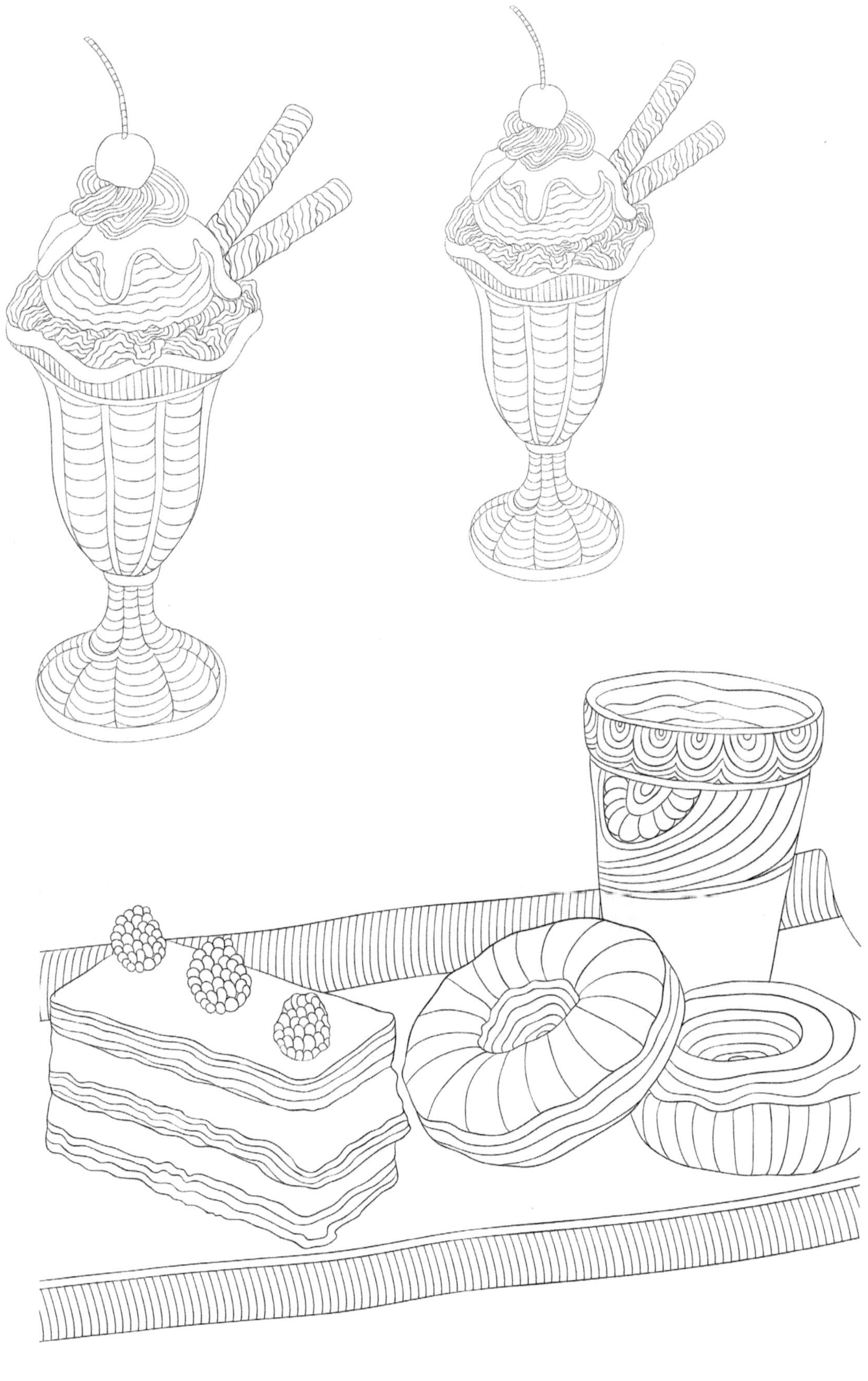

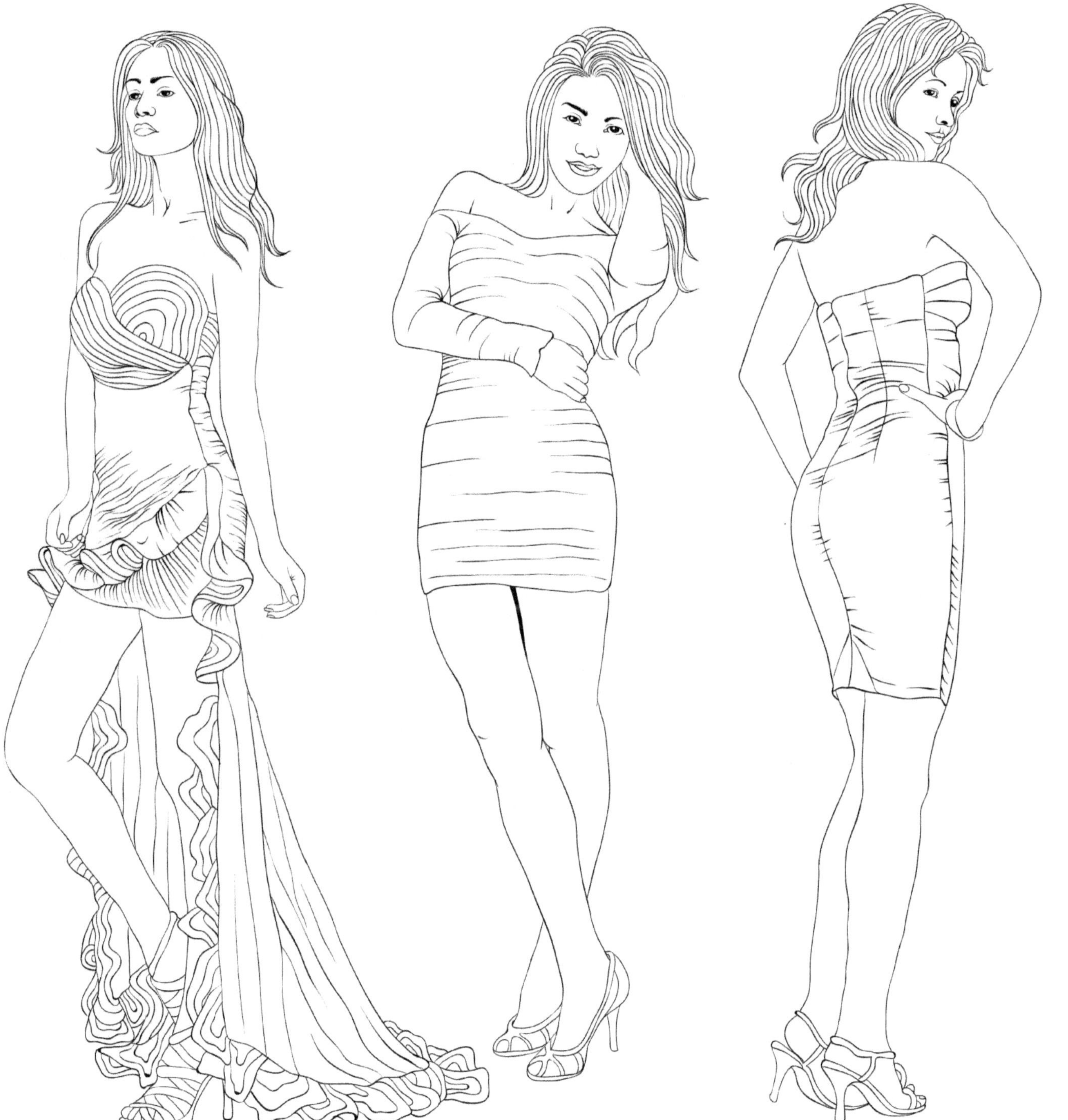

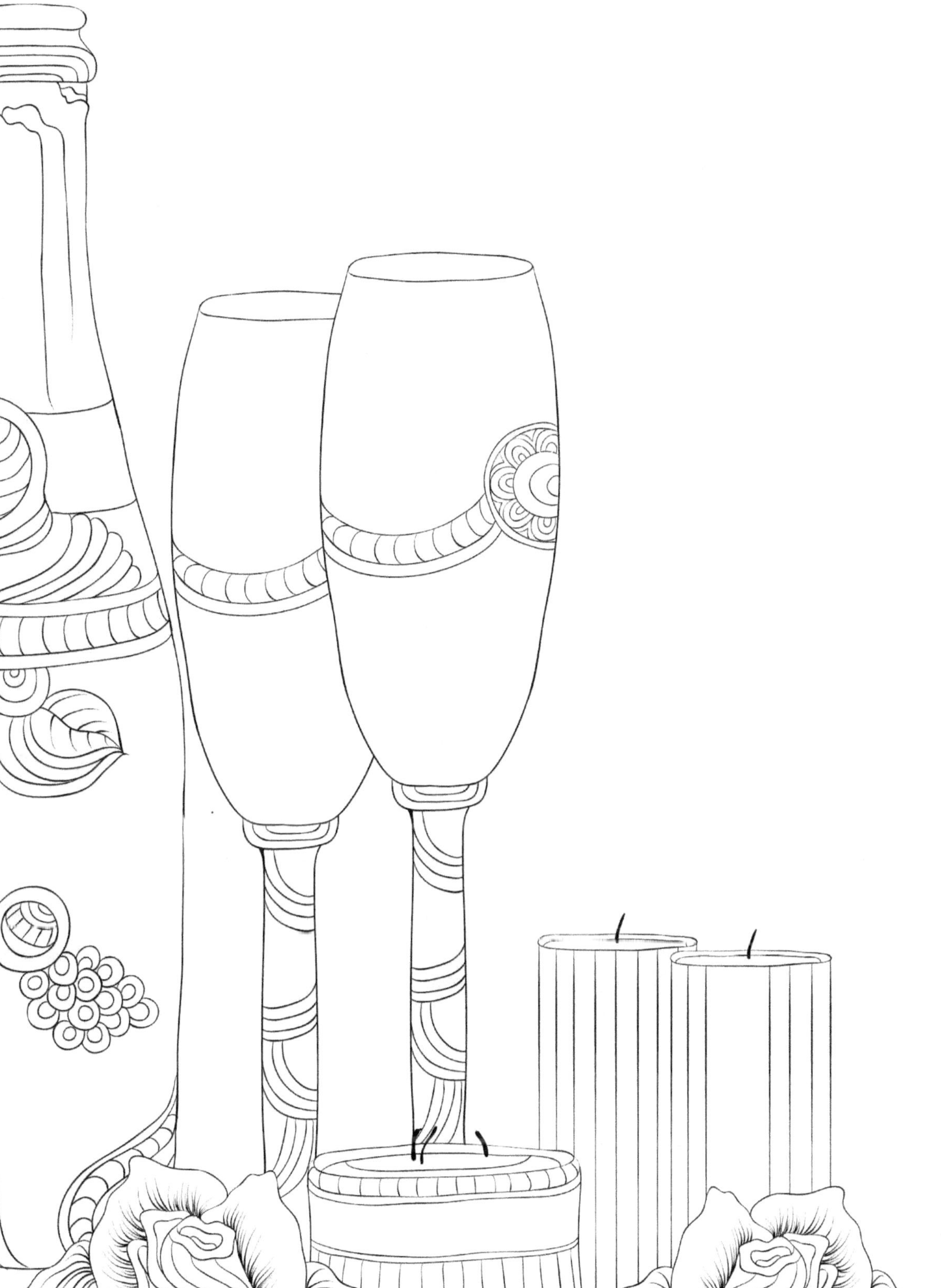

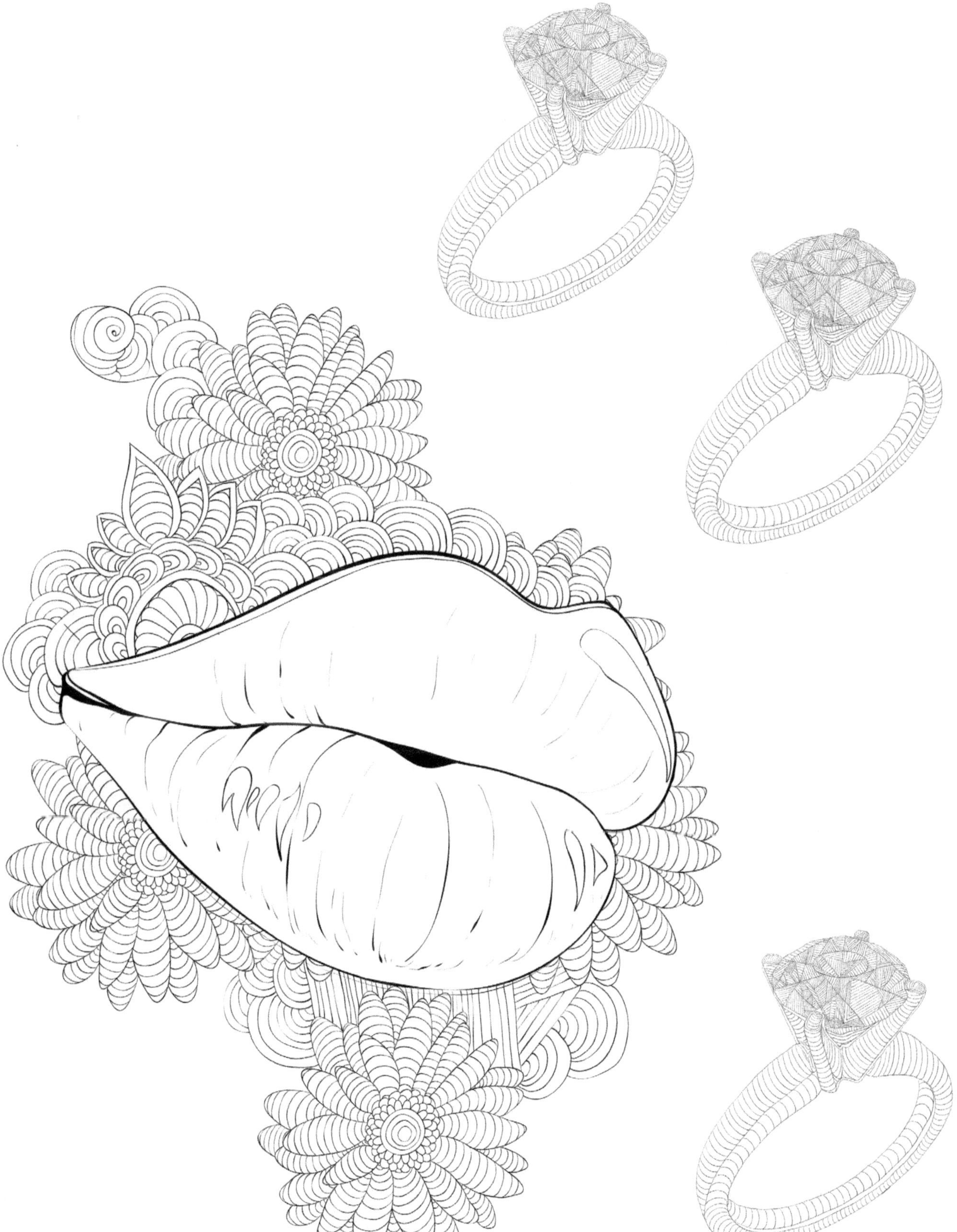

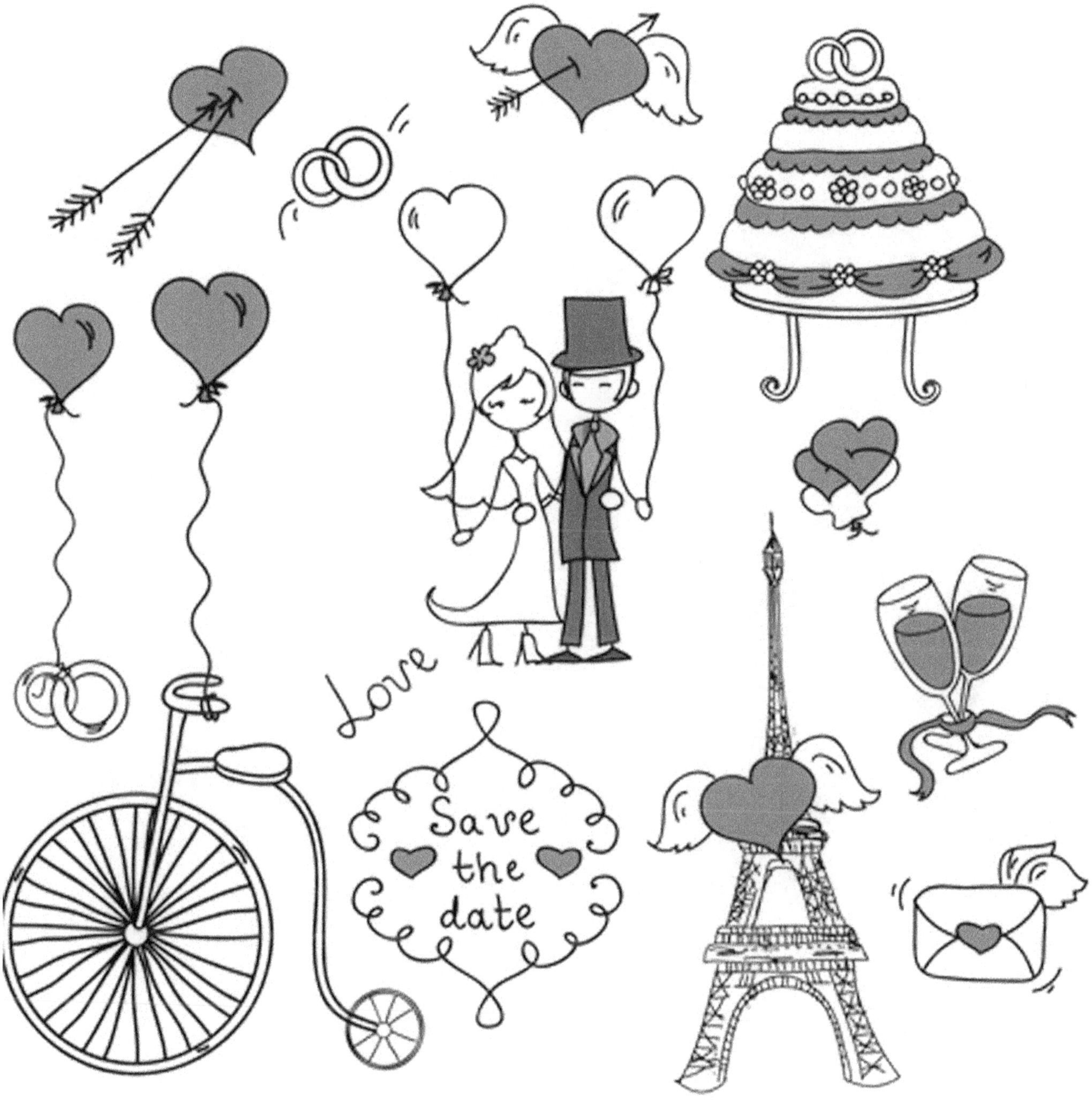
Love
Save
the
date

www.ingramcontent.com/pod-product-compliance
Lightning Source LLC
Chambersburg PA
CBHW080634190526
45169CB00009B/3395
* 9 7 8 1 5 3 0 8 6 4 9 7 3 *